I0815267

Electric Vehicles

How Green Are They?

Carla Mooney

San Diego, CA

About the Author

Carla Mooney is the author of many books for young adults and children. She lives in Pittsburgh, Pennsylvania, with her husband and three children.

Printed in the United States

For more information, contact:
ReferencePoint Press, Inc.
PO Box 27779
San Diego, CA 92198
www.ReferencePointPress.com

Picture Credits:
Cover: Darunrat Wongsuvan/Shutterstock.com

7: jackie ellis/Alamy Stock Photo
10: Mike Flippo/Shutterstock.com
13: Dogora Sun/Shutterstock.com
15: Ian Dewar Photography/Shutterstock.com
19: dpa picture alliance/Alamy Stock Photo
22: Erberto Zani/Alamy Stock Photo
24: Lucas Aguayo Araos/dpa/picture-alliance/Newscom
29: Rudmer Zwerver/Shutterstock.com
31: Quality Stock Arts/Shutterstock.com
36: The Image Party/Shutterstock.com
38: SorbyPhoto/Shutterstock.com
42: Clare Jackson/Alamy Stock Photo
47: Xinhua/Alamy Stock Photo
53: Hazel Plater/Alamy Stock Photo

LIBRARY OF CONGRESS CATALOGING-IN-PUBLICATION DATA

Names: Mooney, Carla- author.
Title Electric Vehicles: How Green Are They?/ by Carla Mooney.
Description: San Diego, CA : ReferencePoint Press, Inc., 2025. | Includes bibliographical references and index.
Identifiers: LCCN 2024018178 (print) | | ISBN 9781678207922 (library binding) | ISBN 978-1678207939 (ebook)
Subjects: LCSH: Climatic changes--Health aspects. | Climatic changes--Health aspects--Juvenile literature. | Health--Juvenile literature.

CONTENTS

Paving the Way for Electric Vehicles

In 2020, the ride-sharing company Uber announced plans to encourage its drivers to use electric vehicles (EVs) when transporting passengers. Uber operates in ten thousand cities worldwide, from Atlanta, Georgia, to Mumbai, India. The company is working to provide 100 percent of rides in EVs in the United States, Canada, and Europe by 2030, with the rest of the world achieving 100 percent electric rides by 2040. "It's our responsibility as the largest mobility platform in the world to more aggressively tackle the challenge of climate change. We want to do our part to build back better and drive a green recovery in our cities,"[1] says Uber chief executive officer Dara Khosrowshahi in a press release.

Uber announced several initiatives to achieve its goal of 100 percent electric rides. It launched a program called Uber Green in select North American cities. Uber Green allows Uber riders to choose to ride in an EV or hybrid vehicle by simply tapping a button in the Uber app. To give riders an incentive to choose EVs, Uber increased reward points for every trip taken in an EV. By January 2024, Uber Green had expanded to more than fourteen hundred cities worldwide, including New York, London, Paris, and San Francisco.

Uber relies on independent contractors as drivers who use their vehicles to provide rides. Uber announced that it was dedicating more than $800 million to help hundreds of thousands of its drivers transition to EVs as part of its EV initiatives.

The company plans to make EVs more attractive to drivers in two significant ways. First, the company pledged to pay drivers of EVs more money with each Uber Green trip completed. The company also teamed up with automakers, charging network providers, and EV rental companies to make buying, renting, and operating an EV more affordable for its drivers. Uber partnered with automakers, including General Motors, Renault, Nissan, and Tesla to extend attractive offers on EVs to drivers. It also worked with rental agencies such as Avis to make renting and testing out EVs easier for drivers. Discounts at charging stations made operating EVs more affordable for its drivers.

By the end of 2023, Uber had seventy-four thousand active EV drivers in the United States, Canada, and Europe. Jack McDonald, a seventy-two-year-old retired college athletics director, is one of Uber's EV drivers. McDonald drives riders around the Boston area in his EV. "It's a brand-new car, and it's climate-friendly. I get a lot of compliments from the riders," says McDonald. In Boston alone, Uber reports that EV drivers have completed 7.1 million miles in zero-emission EVs as of 2023, saving 273,000 gallons (1 million L) of gas. McDonald does not regret his decision to switch to an EV. "It was wiser for me to not spend a lot of money on gas and have a brand-new car that was climate-friendly. I'm still very pleased with having an electric car,"[2] he says.

"It was wiser for me to not spend a lot of money on gas and have a brand-new car that was climate-friendly. I'm still very pleased with having an electric car."[2]

—Jack McDonald, Uber EV driver

Fighting Climate Change

Many have touted EVs as a critical part of the fight against climate change. According to the Natural Resources Defense Council (NRDC), a nonprofit environmental advocacy organization, the transportation industry is the largest source of greenhouse gas emissions in the United States. Burning fossil fuels to power traditional gasoline-powered cars releases greenhouse gas emissions and harmful pollution into the atmosphere. Because EVs do not use fossil fuels, driving EVs eliminates these climate-damaging emissions and pollution. Fossil fuels are also problematic because they are nonrenewable, making it difficult to supply and keep up with increasing demand in the future.

For many drivers, the climate-friendly benefits of EVs are one of the main reasons they choose to purchase an EV. About 72 percent of drivers who were considering buying an EV said that helping the environment was a significant factor in their purchase decision, according to a 2023 survey by Pew Research Center. Akiko Hara from Vancouver, Canada, replaced her gasoline-powered car with an EV because of its environmental benefits:

> When my old Hyundai Elantra received a death sentence at the repair shop in 2019, I decided that my new vehicle was going to be electric. Up until then, I had cared for the Earth by doing small things, such as using reusable grocery bags and recycling plastic and paper products. I wanted to do more. The demise of my gas-powered vehicle presented a perfect opportunity. I looked forward to driving a car that did not emit pollution or run on fossil fuel.[3]

Climate Benefits

Governments and automakers promote EVs as critical for reducing emissions and fighting climate change. Automakers such as General Motors and Volvo have pledged to stop selling gasoline-powered cars and transition to a fully electric portfolio of vehicles. "There is no long-term future for cars with an internal combustion engine," says Henrik Green, Volvo's chief technology officer. "We are firmly committed to becoming an electric-only car maker, and the transition should happen by 2030. It will allow us to meet the expectations of our customers and be a part of the solution when it comes to fighting climate change."[4]

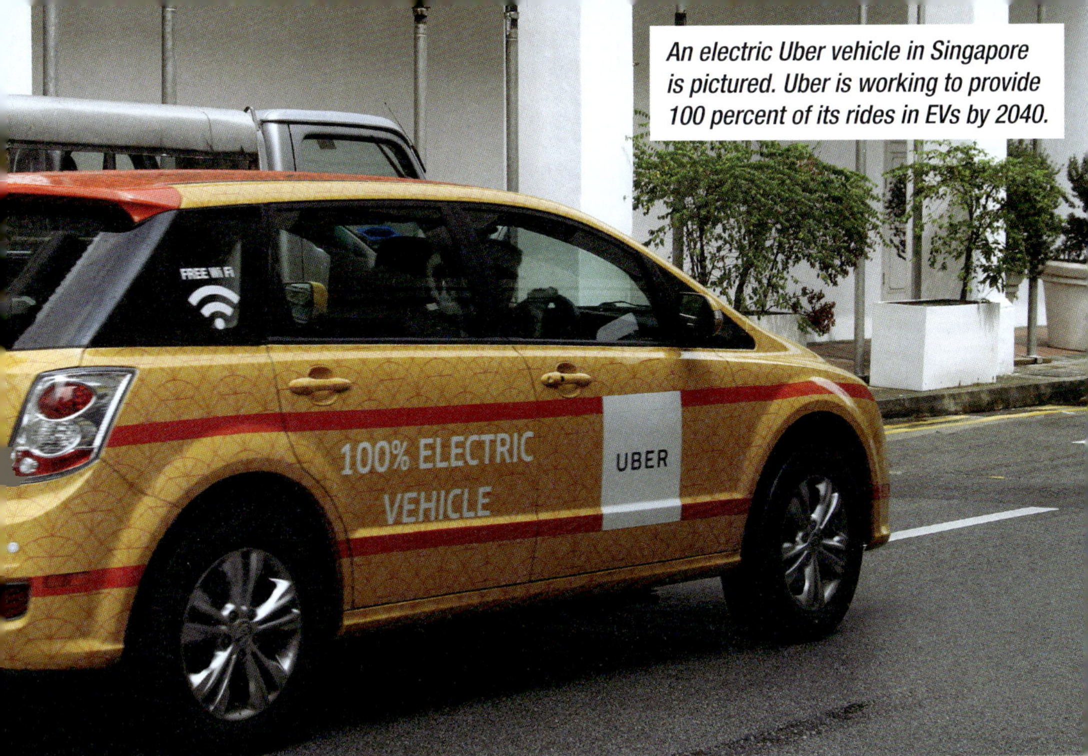

An electric Uber vehicle in Singapore is pictured. Uber is working to provide 100 percent of its rides in EVs by 2040.

However, although experts agree that EVs are more climate friendly to drive than traditional gasoline-powered vehicles, they are not without environmental impacts. The significance of that impact depends on several factors, including how EVs are manufactured and charged and how raw materials for EV batteries are obtained. Graham Conway is a principal engineer for Southwest Research Institute, a nonprofit in San Antonio, Texas, focusing on researching and developing new technologies. According to Conway, evaluations of the "greenness" of EVs must consider emissions released during manufacturing and electricity generation as well as other factors contributing to their ecological footprint. When asked how EVs will impact the environment, Conway says, "The answer is, it depends. That's the only answer I can give you, and stand behind 100 percent. It depends."[5]

Despite such concerns, government agencies and environmental groups are promoting EVs. Although they are not a zero-emission solution, the environmental costs over an EV's lifetime are smaller than that of a traditional vehicle. For this reason, the transition to EVs appears to be a benefit to the environment long-term.

CHAPTER ONE

What Are Electric Vehicles?

Electric cars have existed for decades, but they have become increasingly popular in recent years. In the United States, EVs made up 7.6 percent of new vehicle sales in 2023, according to data from Kelley Blue Book, a car research and valuation company. The number of EVs on the road is projected to increase in the coming years. In some areas, the transition to EVs may happen sooner than in others, as several countries and even some US states have announced initiatives to ban sales of new gasoline-powered vehicles in the next twenty years.

EVs Versus Internal Combustion Engines

Today, most vehicles worldwide are powered by gasoline or diesel fuel. These traditional vehicles have an internal combustion engine that burns gasoline and turns the heat energy into mechanical energy. Mechanical energy moves the vehicle's wheels.

Internal combustion engines work in the same way, whether in a Ford minivan or a Ferrari race car. Inside the engine, pistons move up and down inside metal cylinders. The pistons are connected by rods to a crankshaft. As the pistons move up and down, they spin the crankshaft, which powers the car's wheels and causes them to move. The number of cylinders in a car's engine can vary, but the way they work is the same.

Tiny, controlled explosions create the energy needed to move the engine's pistons up and down. When each piston is in its downward position, the empty chamber above it draws in gasoline and oxygen. As the piston moves upward to fill the chamber, the mixture of gases is compressed. Then, a spark ignites the compressed mixture. When the fuel catches fire, it releases heat and expanding gases that cause each piston to forcefully move downward in the cylinder again. The process repeats and turns the up-and-down motion into rotational motion via the crankshaft. The ignition of the oxygen and gasoline creates carbon dioxide and other gases, which are expelled through the tailpipe.

Unlike gasoline-powered vehicles, most EVs do not use internal combustion engines. Instead, these EVs have an electric motor and rechargeable battery pack. They get energy from plugging into a charging station and storing the electrical energy in a large battery pack. The battery supplies power to the vehicle's motor to move electromagnets that spin the axles and wheels. Because the car does not use gasoline for energy, there is no need for a fuel tank, fuel pump, or fuel line.

Types of EVs

Not all EVs are the same. Some are 100 percent powered by electricity, whereas others use a hybrid system of electricity and gasoline. All-electric EVs, also known as battery-electric vehicles (BEVs), are entirely powered by electricity. BEVs have a large battery pack that holds and provides energy to one or more electric motors that power the car. Popular BEVs include the Chevrolet Bolt EV, Tesla Model 3, and Kia EV6.

Plug-in hybrid electric vehicles (PHEVs) use a large battery to power an electric motor and gasoline to fuel an internal combustion engine. PHEV batteries can be charged by plugging into an electric charging station. These vehicles typically use electric power until the battery is depleted, then the vehicle automatically switches to use the gasoline-powered internal combustion engine.

Hybrid EVs use a combination of electric and gasoline engines. A hybrid electric vehicle is not plugged into an electric charging station to recharge its battery. Instead, the internal combustion engine and regenerative braking recharge the car battery.

EVs get their energy from plugging into a charging station, and then storing the energy in a battery.

Although a hybrid car still uses gasoline in its internal combustion engine, its electric battery provides extra power that can result in less fuel used overall. However, hybrids are not as clean as BEVs and PHEVs.

Growing Popularity

Although EVs are now only a small part of the overall vehicle market in the United States, they are growing in popularity. As of December 2023, approximately 3 million EVs were on the road in the United States, according to an Experian Automotive Market Trends report. That number increased from 2 million EVs in 2022 and 1.3 million EVs in 2021.

Industry experts project the number of EVs on the road will continue to increase in the coming years. Recent sales statistics back up these projections. In 2023, according to data from Kelley Blue Book, nearly 1.2 million US vehicle buyers chose EVs over gasoline-powered cars. EVs were the fastest-growing car sales category in 2023, making up a 7.6 share of 2023 new car sales, compared to 5.9 percent in 2022. "Americans bought a record-shattering 1,189,051 electric vehicles (EVs) [in 2023], and we expect that growth to continue into the future," says Stephanie Valdez Streaty, a director at Cox Automotive, an automobile services company. "The momentum is strong for more when it comes to EVs—more new product, more incentives, more inventory, more leasing, and more infrastructure—and that momentum is not going away. . . . Our team forecasts that EV share of the total U.S. market will reach 10% in 2024."[6]

"Americans bought a record-shattering 1,189,051 electric vehicles (EVs) [in 2023], and we expect that growth to continue into the future."[6]

—Stephanie Valdez Streaty, a director at Cox Automotive

The Environmental Benefits of EVs

Replacing gasoline-powered vehicles with EVs has numerous environmental benefits. Burning fossil fuel to power a traditional car releases greenhouse gases into Earth's atmosphere. Greenhouse gases trap heat in Earth's atmosphere, which is causing global warming. As Earth's atmosphere, surface, and oceans warm, its climate is changing. Climate changes have triggered many problems for people worldwide, from extreme weather to rising seas.

The transportation industry is the largest source of greenhouse gas emissions, according to the NRDC. In the United States, traditional gasoline-powered vehicles release about 1.5 billion tons (1.4 billion t) of greenhouse gases into Earth's atmosphere annu-

Regenerative Braking

Most EVs sold in the United States are equipped with a regenerative braking system. In a traditional car, a hydraulic braking system uses friction to slow a moving car. Rubbing the car's brake pads against the brake disc produces friction and converts the car's kinetic energy of movement into heat. This heat from friction is not captured or used. In comparison, a regenerative braking system uses that heat energy to recharge its battery and provide a little more driving range. Over time, the recaptured energy can add up to significant benefits. However, one drawback of regenerative braking is that it is not as reliable when a car is traveling at high speeds. Therefore, EVs typically have both types of braking systems.

ally, mainly as carbon dioxide, according to the US Department of Energy. Each gallon of gasoline burned in a traditional vehicle releases about 20 pounds (9 kg) of greenhouse gases. These emissions add up to approximately 5 to 9 tons (4.5 to 8.2 t) of greenhouse gas emissions annually for the average vehicle. In comparison, BEVs and PHEVs running on electricity release no greenhouse gas emissions. EVs are a cleaner alternative to fossil-fuel-powered vehicles.

EVs Reduce Pollution

Vehicles that burn fossil fuels emit harmful gases and particulates into the air. "Most air pollution comes from energy use and production,"[7] says John Walke, director of the clean air team at the NRDC.

Air pollution and particulates from vehicles cause a variety of health problems. Air pollution can make it harder to breathe, cause wheezing and coughing, and trigger asthma attacks, bronchitis, or other respiratory conditions. Breathing in air pollution also increases the risk of respiratory infections, cancer, heart disease, and stroke. "The less gasoline we burn, the better we're doing to reduce air pollution and the harmful effects of climate change. Make good choices about transportation. When you can, ride a bike, walk, or take public transportation. For driving, choose a car that gets better miles per gallon of gas or buy an electric car,"[8] says Walke.

Air pollution is also responsible for millions of worldwide deaths annually. In a 2023 study, an international team of scientists created a new model to estimate deaths caused by air pollution from fossil fuels. The model estimated fossil-fuel-caused air pollution was responsible for 5.1 million avoidable deaths. "Major reductions in air pollution emissions, notably through a phaseout of fossil fuels, could have large, positive health outcomes. Results show that the mortality burden attributable to air pollution from fossil fuel use

> **"The less gasoline we burn, the better we're doing to reduce air pollution and the harmful effects of climate change."[8]**
>
> **—John Walke, director of the NRDC's clean air team**

Cars driving on a freeway in San Diego, California. Vehicles that burn fossil fuels emit harmful pollution and particulates into the air.

is higher than most previous estimates,"[9] the global team of researchers wrote.

EVs can also reduce the world's reliance on nonrenewable resources. Fossil fuels are limited, and their supply eventually will be exhausted. In contrast, renewable energy sources such as the sun and wind are unlimited and naturally replenished. When renewable energy generates electricity to power EVs, demand for nonrenewable fossil fuels will decline even more.

More to the Story

Most experts agree that EVs are better for the environment than vehicles with internal combustion engines. But EVs are not emissions- or pollution-free. From the start, mining and processing the raw materials needed to produce EV batteries is energy intensive. Much of the energy used comes from emissions-producing fossil fuels. Mining operations can also contaminate the local environment with toxic waste, and there are rising concerns about human rights violations at many mining sites.

The manufacturing process for EV batteries also releases greenhouse gas emissions and pollution. Battery manufacturing facilities typically use fossil fuels to generate the high heat needed to work with the metals used in EV batteries. Overall, EV production creates more harmful emissions and pollution than the production of traditional vehicles.

Although driving an EV is cleaner than driving a gasoline-powered car, it is not entirely emissions-free. Today, most electricity that powers EVs comes from power plants, many of which use fossil fuels to generate electricity. As they produce electricity, these power plants release greenhouse gases and pollution into the atmosphere.

However, experts note that even when using electricity generated by fossil fuels, EVs are still cleaner to operate, and release fewer greenhouse gases than a traditional vehicle. "An electric vehicle running on [electricity generated with] coal has the fuel economy equivalent in the order of about 50 to 60 miles [80 to 97 km] per gallon equivalent. So the dirtiest electric vehicle looks

The History of Electric Vehicles

Around 1890, a chemist named William Morrison in Des Moines, Iowa, made the first successful electric car in the United States. His six-passenger vehicle could travel 14 miles per hour (23 kmh) and sparked early interest in EVs. Over the next decade, different automakers created their version of the EV. By 1900, EVs were one-third of all cars on the road. New York City had more than sixty electric taxis. Although horses were still the most popular transportation choice, Americans embraced the new motor vehicles powered by steam, gasoline, or electricity. Many liked electric cars because they were quiet and easy to drive. Particularly in urban areas, EVs worked well for short trips on city roads. In 1908, however, Henry Ford introduced his mass-produced gasoline-powered car, the Model T. The Model T was widely available and affordable for the average American. Additionally, the availability of Texas crude oil made gas cheap and accessible, and gas stations popped up across the country. In comparison, electricity was not widely available outside of cities. For these reasons, Americans increasingly chose gasoline-powered cars. By 1935, EVs had mostly disappeared across the country.

A wind farm in southern Washington produces electricity for the surrounding population. As more of the electricity needed by EVs is generated by renewable energy sources like this, EVs will be cleaner to operate.

something like our best gasoline vehicles that are available today,"[10] says David Keith, an assistant professor of system dynamics at the Massachusetts Institute of Technology (MIT).

Keith notes that as more renewable energy sources are used to generate the electricity needed by EVs, the EVs will be cleaner to operate. These benefits are already seen in areas where renewable sources produce more electricity. "In New England or the Pacific Northwest, the fuel economy equivalent of an EV is into the hundreds: 110–120 miles [177 to 193 km] per gallon equivalent,"[11] says Keith.

Life Cycle Analysis

EVs have drawn a lot of attention as a sustainable solution to transportation. Their appeal primarily comes from their lack of greenhouse gas emissions compared to traditional cars. However, emissions are only part of the EV story. To fully understand the impact of EVs on the environment, scientists caution that

> “We shouldn’t claim victory that with this switch to electric cars, problem solved, we are going to have zero emissions. No, that’s not the case. But electric cars are actually much, much better in terms of the impact on the climate in comparison to internal combustion vehicles.”[12]
>
> —Sergey Paltsev, a senior research scientist at MIT

emissions and other effects from the entire vehicle life cycle must be considered, including manufacturing, operation, and end of life. Each EV life cycle step, from mining raw materials to end-of-life battery disposal, is linked to greenhouse gas emissions and contributes to its sustainability.

Even using a life cycle analysis, scientists agree that EVs are greener than traditional vehicles. A 2022 analysis from the Union of Concerned Scientists found that the average BEV produces 50 percent fewer greenhouse gases over its lifetime—from manufacturing to disposal—than a comparable gasoline-powered vehicle. “We shouldn’t claim victory that with this switch to electric cars, problem solved, we are going to have zero emissions. No, that’s not the case. But electric cars are actually much, much better in terms of the impact on the climate in comparison to internal combustion vehicles. And in time, that comparative advantage of electric cars is going to grow,”[12] says Sergey Paltsev, a senior research scientist at MIT.

Mining for Raw Materials

As interest in EVs has increased, the production of EV batteries and their impact on the environment has come under increased scrutiny. Electric vehicles rely on large lithium-ion batteries to provide the power they need to run. Lithium-ion batteries offer several advantages for EVs. However, they also come with several environmental and ethical challenges. "If you are going to take a look at any source of energy, you always will have some trade-offs. There is no magic solution,"[13] says MIT's Paltsev.

The Benefits of Lithium-Ion Batteries

Lithium-ion batteries have several qualities that make them a good choice for use in EVs. They are small and light but also powerful. Lithium-ion batteries have a high energy density, which means they can store large amounts of electrical energy in a smaller, lighter package than other types of batteries. "A lithium-metal battery is considered the holy grail for battery chemistry because of its high capacity and energy density,"[14] says Xin Li, an associate professor of materials science at Harvard. Lithium-ion batteries also are fast charging and use a charger that can determine when the battery is fully charged.

Unlike some batteries that become less effective over time, lithium-ion batteries hold up well to repeated charging and use. They retain almost all their original storage capacity, even after being charged and used many times. Also, this type of battery has a low self-discharge rate, which means it can hold its stored energy even if it is not in regular use. That feature is essential in EVs because it means a car that has not been driven for several weeks will still be able to start. Lithium-ion batteries also perform well at both high and low temperatures.

Concerns About Raw Materials

Lithium-ion batteries are made from raw materials, including lithium, cobalt, nickel, manganese, and graphite. According to MIT researchers, the average EV battery uses six times more minerals than a conventional vehicle, excluding steel and aluminum. Extracting these minerals can harm the environment, potentially causing soil degradation, water shortages, biodiversity loss, ecosystem damage, and pollution.

Also, several minerals used in lithium-ion batteries have been categorized as critical minerals by the US government. Critical minerals are essential to US economic or national security and have a supply chain at risk of disruption. Although critical minerals exist worldwide, the most viable sources are only found in a few locations. For example, lithium is mainly found in South America and Australia, and cobalt is concentrated in the Democratic Republic of the Congo (DRC) in Africa. Also, minerals are finite resources. In addition, mining and processing the minerals for EV batteries can present ethical and safety challenges, such as using child labor and inadequate safety measures for workers.

Cobalt Mining

Cobalt is a hard, silver-gray metal. Found in Earth's crust, cobalt must be extracted from its ore, a mixture of natural rock or sediment and valuable minerals. Most of the cobalt supply is extracted from existing industrial copper and cobalt mines run by large mining companies.

Approximately 70 percent of the world's cobalt supply is produced in the DRC, Africa's second-largest country. The DRC is also home to much of the Congo Basin, a river drainage region

A worker at a battery factory in Germany moves an EV lithium-ion battery during testing. Electric vehicles rely on lithium-ion batteries for power.

engulfed by the world's second-largest tropical rain forest. The Congo Basin also holds the world's largest tropical peatlands, which store about 29 billion tons (26 billion t) of carbon. The entire Congo Basin absorbs almost 1.5 billion tons (1.4 billion t) of carbon dioxide from the atmosphere each year. As a result, scientists believe it has a vital role in the battle against climate change because it acts as a carbon sink that keeps this tremendous amount of carbon dioxide from entering the atmosphere. "The Congo Basin is one of the world's last regions that absorbs more carbon than it emits. We have to find ways to meet critical energy needs for development without sacrificing peatlands and the essential services they provide for people and the economy,"[15] says Doreen Robinson of the United Nations Environment Programme.

As the demand for cobalt has increased in recent years, legal and illegal cobalt mines have appeared across the DRC. Mining

Problems with Nickel

Nickel is an essential element used in lithium-ion batteries. Using nickel in the cathodes of lithium-ion batteries improves performance and storage capacity. However, mining nickel has numerous environmental costs, including water use and greenhouse gas emissions. In nickel mining, nickel ores are mined from the ground, crushed, and added to significant amounts of water to separate the nickel from waste materials. Waste from this process can drain into nearby surface and groundwater, contaminating water sources, damaging ecosystems and human health.

On the Indonesian island of Obi, a large nickel mining operation has cleared the hills of trees and left deep gouges in the earth. Along the island's coast, ocean water has turned from a shimmering aquamarine to a dull, reddish brown. Scientists have detected the presence of heavy metals in fish caught off Obi's shores. If eaten by humans, these fish pose a risk to health. Mining operations have also contributed to habitat destruction from deforestation and air pollution. Once extracted, nickel processing releases toxic sulfur dioxide and particulates into the air, particularly in coal-fired nickel smelters. People living near nickel mines and smelting operations have reported higher rates of respiratory issues and other pollution-related health problems.

operations have threatened the rainforest and the biodiverse species that live there. Millions of trees have been cleared for mining operations. Deforestation has destroyed valuable natural habitats and threatened the biodiversity that relies on the Congo Basin.

The DRC, like many places with cobalt reserves, has limited environmental regulations around mining activity. As a result, mining operations have released waste and other pollutants that have contaminated nearby rivers and land. This has reduced access to clean drinking water and food sources. "In this stream, the fish vanished long ago, killed by acids and waste from the mines,"[16] says Congo resident Heritier Maloba about his childhood fishing hole. Studies of fish collected from lakes near mining operations have revealed that many fish are contaminated with toxic substances, including cobalt, manganese, and uranium. When humans eat contaminated fish, the toxins can threaten their health.

Cobalt mining also releases toxic pollutants. Dust and grit from crushing rock make the air hazy and cause breathing problems for people living nearby. Additionally, metals are extracted through smelting, which releases sulfur dioxide and other pollutants into the air. Scientists worry that long-term exposure to these toxins, in particular uranium, which is released during the mining process, will cause lung disease and other health conditions. "The uranium also releases a gas called radon gas, and in the mines, the radon levels are very very high. Radon is a carcinogen that could lead to lung cancer. But we don't know to what extent there is an increased amount of lung cancer in the area because it's an underserved area medically,"[17] says Belgian pulmonary specialist Benoit Nemery.

Concerns over Human Rights

Although most cobalt is produced in the DRC's industrial mines, approximately 15 to 30 percent of the global cobalt supply is produced in artisanal mines. Artisanal miners work for themselves or for small enterprises that do not have the resources or labor and safety concerns associated with regulated companies. These workers typically dig by hand in makeshift pits. An estimated two hundred thousand people in the DRC work in artisanal and small-scale mining operations. There are significant human rights concerns about the conditions in these mines. "We shouldn't be transitioning to the use of electric vehicles at the cost of the people and environment of one of the most downtrodden and impoverished corners of the world. The bottom of the supply chain, where almost all the world's cobalt is coming from, is a horror show,"[18] says Siddharth Kara, a Harvard fellow who has researched modern-day slavery and child labor.

> **"We shouldn't be transitioning to the use of electric vehicles at the cost of the people and environment of one of the most downtrodden and impoverished corners of the world. The bottom of the supply chain, where almost all the world's cobalt is coming from, Is a horror show."[18]**
>
> **—Siddharth Kara, a Harvard researcher**

Artisanal miners dig cobalt from the ground, usually for only a few dollars a day. The mines where they work are often dangerous and offer little protection for workers. Miners do not have

This photo shows illegal mining in the Democratic Republic of Congo in Africa. This work is often dangerous.

protective equipment like vests and hard hats. Instead, they usually work barefoot and dig cobalt ore by hand. "People are working in subhuman, grinding, degrading conditions. They use pickaxes, shovels, stretches of rebar to hack and scrounge at the earth in trenches and pits and tunnels to gather cobalt,"[19] says Kara.

Without adequate protection, hundreds of miners have died or been injured in mine collapses and other mining accidents. Others suffer from chemical exposures, breathing toxic dust, and injuries from lifting and carrying heavy loads. "Cobalt is toxic to touch and breathe—and there are hundreds of thousands of poor Congolese people touching and breathing it day in and day out. Young mothers with babies strapped to their backs, all breathing in this toxic cobalt dust,"[20] says Kara.

"The [Congolese] government doesn't provide money for schools, so parents send their children to the mines instead."[21]

—Albert Mutawa, a manager of an artisanal mine in the DRC

Also, artisanal mines often rely on child labor. Many children work in these unsafe environments, putting themselves at risk of injury and abuse to help their families pay for basic needs. "The government doesn't provide money for schools, so parents send their children to the mines instead,"[21] says Albert Mutawa, a manager of an artisanal mine.

Mining Lithium

Lithium is another essential raw material used in EV batteries. Lithium is a soft, silvery metal that forms in salty underground waters, hard rock, or clay. Its reactivity and lightness allow EVs to generate energy and speed similar to gasoline-powered cars. Most of the world's lithium supply is produced in Australia or South America's "lithium triangle," an area of salt flats in Argentina, Bolivia, and Chile.

Extracting lithium, no matter where it forms, is a water-intensive process. One method involves blasting lithium-rich ore from open pits. Another method, called brine mining, extracts lithium from brine, or salty underground water. The salty liquid is pumped to the surface into pools where the water evaporates, leaving behind lithium and other minerals.

Lithium mining has environmental costs. Mining can disturb landscapes and habitats, and waste from mining operations, including toxic chemicals and minerals, contaminate nearby communities' water supplies. Additionally, mining lithium requires sig-

A Lithium Deposit in Thacker Pass

Scientists from Columbia University have discovered a significant lithium deposit on the border of Nevada and Oregon. The discovery was made in a volcanic crater in an area known as Thacker Pass. The deposit could potentially be the largest lithium deposit in the world, holding up to 120 million tons (109 million t) of the mineral. Mining of the deposit could begin as early as 2026. However, conservationists are attempting to block mining in the area, citing threats to ecosystems and potential violations of environmental laws. Native American activists have also protested mining in the region because Thacker Pass is a sacred place for several local tribes. They filed a federal lawsuit to halt construction of the open-pit lithium mine. However, in November 2023, a federal judge ruled against three Native American tribes and allowed the construction of the mine to proceed.

nificant amounts of freshwater, a resource that can be scarce in certain mining areas. Water is used to separate minerals, cool machinery, and control dust. The amount of water required for lithium mining makes producing EVs approximately 50 percent more water intensive than manufacturing traditional internal combustion vehicles, according to a 2020 report by the Congressional Research Service.

Brine mining is particularly water intensive. In South America, over half of the world's lithium supply can be found in underground brine pools beneath the area's extensive salt flats. In the brine mining process, about 500,000 gallons (1.9 million L) of brine water are pumped and evaporated to extract 1 ton (0.9 t) of lithium. In some cases, pumping out such large amounts of brine water has caused freshwater to flow into brine aquifers, where it mixes with saltwater. As a result, the freshwater becomes salty and unfit for drinking or agricultural use, and nearby freshwater and groundwater supplies are depleted.

A brine pool in Atacama, Chile. Brine mining is one way to extract lithium from the ground, but it often depletes and contaminates freshwater supplies.

In Salar de Atacama, one of Chile's central mining regions, lithium and copper mining has used more than 65 percent of the local water supply, leaving little usable water for local farming communities. As lithium mining operations deplete local water sources, communities rely on tankers to deliver usable water for daily life. "Chile is going through a tremendous water crisis," says Elena Rivera Cardoso, president of the Indigenous Colla community of the Copiapó commune in northern Chile. "We used to have a river before that now doesn't exist. There isn't a drop of water. And not only here in Copiapó but in all of Chile, there are rivers and lakes that have disappeared—all because a company has a lot more right to water than we do as human beings or citizens of Chile."[22]

Responsible Sourcing of Materials

As the demand for EVs rises, the need for EV batteries and the minerals used in them will also increase. Demand for cobalt is expected to increase twentyfold by 2040, according to the International Energy Agency. Lithium demand is projected to increase fortyfold by 2040, according to the NRDC. To improve the sustainability of EVs, scientists will need to develop ways to reduce or eliminate the need for problematic raw materials. Several automakers have pledged to source cobalt responsibly and not buy from mines that use child labor. Scientists are also working to develop EV batteries that eliminate the need for cobalt.

However, until then, EV battery manufacturers must work with existing mines to improve worker health and safety and lessen mining's impact on local communities and the environment. If raw materials like cobalt and lithium can be extracted responsibly, the increasing demand for EVs will be more economically favorable and less problematic for communities where these minerals are found. If not, "they will put the environment and many, many miners' lives at risk,"[23] says Mickaël Daudin of Pact, a nonprofit organization that advocates for Africa's mining communities.

CHAPTER THREE

The Electric Vehicle Production Process

Though EVs have an ecological advantage over internal combustion engine vehicles in terms of vehicle operation, the production process, especially in producing EV batteries, adds to an EV's overall carbon footprint. Mining, processing, and manufacturing EV batteries require significant energy, which can generate substantial amounts of greenhouse gas emissions. As a result, before an EV hits the road for the first time, it already has a significant carbon footprint.

Manufacturing EV Batteries

The minerals used in EV batteries are extracted from the earth and refined for use. The mined ore is almost never pure. It needs to be refined and processed before it can be used to build batteries. Mining and refining equipment are often powered by fossil fuels, generating significant greenhouse gas emissions. Transporting minerals from mines to processing facilities and manufacturing plants often uses fossil fuel–powered vehicles that generate greenhouse gas emissions every mile traveled.

Manufacturing an EV's large lithium-ion battery generates a significant part of total EV emissions because industrial plants require energy to operate. Battery production typically generates 40 to 60 percent of total EV production emissions, according to a 2023 McKinsey & Company report. "Making batteries can generate as much emissions as producing all the other materials that go into making an EV—or even more,"[24] the authors wrote.

Lithium-ion batteries have three main components: cells, a battery management system, and a pack. Within each lithium-ion battery, many smaller cells contain the battery's active materials. Each cell contains two electrodes, called the anode and cathode, and an electrolyte solution. The lithium-ion battery generates power when electrons move from the cell's anode through an electrolyte solution to the cathode. Anodes are typically made of metals such as graphite or zinc, and cathodes are often made from lithium oxide. The electrolyte is typically a lithium salt solution that transports electrons. Manufacturers link multiple cells to build a larger battery and create the needed electrical voltage. The battery management system controls the battery's performance and safety, and the pack is the structure in which the individual cells are mounted.

The production process for lithium-ion batteries is very energy intensive, and manufacturing the battery's cells is the most energy-intensive part. Up to 75 percent of the energy required to make the battery is used to produce the cells. Some steps in the production process require intense heat of between 1,472°F and 1,832°F (800°C and 1,000°C). In these steps, boilers and electricity are used to form precipitates, which then have to be dried by exposing them to strong heat for several hours. Burning fossil fuels is the easiest and most inexpensive way to achieve such high temperatures.

Energy Sources Matter

Emissions from battery manufacturing can vary greatly depending on where they are made and the energy sources used to power factories. When renewable energy sources power factories, emissions are low. However, most of the world's electric power plants still burn fossil fuels, generating significant greenhouse gas emissions.

Even the choice of fossil fuel can have an impact on emissions. For example, burning coal emits approximately twice the amount of greenhouse gases as natural gas, another fossil fuel frequently used in electric power plants. Today, 80 percent of the world's lithium-ion batteries are manufactured in China, including almost 60 percent of EV batteries. China powers its battery manufacturing primarily with coal, a dirty fossil fuel. In comparison, European power plants typically rely less on fossil fuels and more on nuclear and hydropower. Manufacturing processes that use fewer fossil fuels produce fewer carbon dioxide emissions.

Transporting batteries from production sites to final destinations can also generate greenhouse gas emissions. The amount of emissions depends on the distance traveled, the type of transportation used, and the energy used to power transportation. For example, shipping lithium-ion batteries on a fossil-fuel-powered ship from China to the United States generates carbon emissions that should be considered when evaluating the climate impact of EVs.

> **"If you look at the data, that 'carbon debt' is paid off within about two years of driving the vehicle."[25]**
>
> —Eoin Devane, a senior climate science adviser in the United Kingdom

Overall, the production of EVs generates about 60 percent more carbon emissions than the production of traditional cars and trucks, according to a 2022 analysis by the Argonne National Laboratory in Illinois. As a result, EVs coming off the production line have a larger carbon footprint, or carbon debt, than traditional vehicles. However, that disadvantage is quickly reduced and eliminated because the EV drives emissions-free. "If you look at the data, that 'carbon debt' is paid off within about two years of driving the vehicle,"[25] says Eoin Devane, a senior climate science adviser with the United Kingdom's Climate Change Committee.

Scientists are developing new EV manufacturing processes and battery chemistries that are more climate friendly and use more sustainable materials. However, these technologies are not yet ready to be implemented widely in EV production. Many scientists believe that improvements in how EVs and their batteries are sourced and produced will be critical for achieving their green potential. "If we don't change how we make materials, how we make

Industrial plants require energy to operate, and creating that energy can also cause pollution. This picture shows emissions from a coal-powered electricity plant.

chemicals, how we manufacture, everything will essentially stay the same,"[26] says Yang Shao-Horn, professor of engineering at MIT.

Disposal Concerns

Although lithium-ion batteries perform well for many charging cycles, a battery's performance will eventually deteriorate to the point that it will need to be replaced. The disposal of used lithium-ion batteries creates another challenge for the environment. If not handled properly, the disposal of used batteries can harm the environment. Many small lithium-ion batteries are thrown away and end up in landfills. Batteries dumped in landfills can leak toxins into nearby soil and groundwater, including cobalt, manganese, nickel, and lithium salts.

In addition, flammable materials in lithium-ion batteries can cause landfill fires and explosions. These fires can burn for extended periods and release toxic chemicals into the air. In Alabama, an underground landfill fire burned for more than four years, releasing toxins that polluted the air for miles and sickened many people in local communities.

Gigafactories

Most lithium-ion batteries for EVs are manufactured in massive plants termed gigafactories. A gigafactory usually makes components for industries and products that are moving toward electrification. Electrification occurs when fossil fuel technologies, such as internal combustion engines, are replaced with electric-powered technologies, such as EVs. For the automotive industry, gigafactories initially produced lithium-ion batteries to power EVs. However, they have expanded to include nearly every part of manufacturing EVs. Gigafactories produce batteries, electronic components, EVs, and the equipment needed to charge them.

In Oregon's landfills and recycling centers, exploding lithium-ion batteries have triggered numerous fires. In Oregon's Deschutes County, the local landfill previously experienced battery fires about once a month, but now it is reporting battery fires multiple times per week. In 2023, the landfill reported twenty-one lithium-related fires over three months, according to Tim Brownell, the Deschutes County solid waste director. "(Lithium batteries) are everywhere in the system. It's a public safety concern and it's a concern for the infrastructure that are taxpayer investments,"[27] says Brownell.

> "The least wasteful and polluting mine is a mine that is never built."[29]
>
> —Jordan Brinn, an expert on transportation electrification policy at the NRDC

The fires sometimes start before the battery arrives at the landfill. Garbage trucks have arrived at the landfills with a battery-related fire smoldering in the back. The bigger the battery, the bigger the fires, according to Brownell. "You might get flames that are three or four feet up in the air. Once you get flames like that, you start to get concerned about it starting to catch the adjacent materials around it,"[28] says Brownell.

Recycling Used Batteries

Recycling lithium-ion batteries has the potential to offset some of the environmental impact of producing EVs. Recycling enables manufacturers to reuse raw materials in new batteries and decrease the need to mine new minerals. "The least wasteful and polluting mine is a mine that is never built,"[29] says Jordan Brinn, an expert on transportation electrification policy at the NRDC. Less raw material mining ultimately leads to fewer emissions, pollution, and other harms related to mining and refining operations. Recycling can also reduce the environmental risks of disposing of lithium-ion batteries. However, recycling efforts will need to increase to impact the environment significantly. Currently, only about 5 percent of lithium-ion batteries are recycled worldwide. In comparison, approximately 99 percent of lead-acid car batteries are recycled.

To become more widespread, EV battery recycling must overcome several barriers. One barrier is that recycling EV batteries is very difficult and costly. To be recycled, the EV batteries must first be taken apart, which is challenging and dangerous. If a battery is cut in the wrong place, it can short-circuit, catch on fire, and release toxic fumes. EV batteries are also not standardized. Batteries from Tesla, Nissan, and BMW are of different sizes and contain different-shaped battery cells that are welded together in

A pile of used EV car batteries. Only a small percentage of lithium-ion batteries are recycled worldwide.

different ways. Battery cells are often joined together with tough glues that are difficult to remove. "The significant challenge in battery recycling is the variability in chemistry and form . . . and that we have to be cautious to discharge them when they are recovered,"[30] says Elsa Olivetti, a professor of engineering at MIT.

> **"On the one side, [disposing of EV batteries] is a waste management problem. And on the other side, it's an opportunity for producing a sustainable secondary stream of critical materials."[31]**
>
> **—Gavin Harper, a University of Birmingham researcher**

Despite these challenges, better recycling of used EV batteries could not only reduce environmental harms but also help countries improve economic and national security. Currently, the supply of critical battery materials is controlled by only a few countries. Recycling increases the supply of these materials and gives countries more control over their supply chain. "On the one side, [disposing of EV batteries] is a waste management problem. And on the other side, it's an opportunity for producing a sustainable secondary stream of critical materials,"[31] says Gavin Harper, an EV policy researcher at the UK's University of Birmingham.

Once the battery has been taken apart, there are several potential methods to recycle its materials. Some processes use high-heat furnaces to recover some of the battery's metals. Other processes use chemical solutions dissolved in water to pull out the metals. Neither method is without cost. Using high heat requires a lot of energy, and chemical processes are very time-consuming. In some cases, it is cheaper for a manufacturer to buy new materials instead of using recycled materials.

In Fredrikstad, Norway, a former steel plant has been transformed into a battery recycling center. After workers take apart battery packs, a machine shreds the packs and separates plastic, aluminum, and copper from a powdery black mass. The black mass contains minerals, including lithium, nickel, cobalt, manganese, and graphite. It is processed to retrieve battery-grade materials that can be used in the manufacture of new batteries. Established in 2020, the Hydrovolt factory is the first of several battery recycling centers planned for Europe and the United States. The factory partners with car manufacturers, battery manufacturers, and auto scrap dealers. The company's website states that

> by pioneering battery recycling of EVs and industrial batteries, we create a circular solution for batteries at their end-of-life by enabling production of high quality, and sustainable, raw materials. At Hydrovolt, a battery can become a battery an infinite number of times. We do this to ensure that no battery is ever wasted by enabling urban mining through our vision of completely clean electrification.[32]

Repurpose and Reuse

Reusing EV batteries is another possible way to keep them out of landfills. EV batteries that no longer support long-distance driving could be repurposed for other energy storage needs. For example, old EV batteries could be repurposed to store energy and provide backup electricity to the power grid. "But we have to be sure we understand the state of the battery's health," Olivetti says. "And that's a challenge."[33]

Recycling Metals

To recover metals from EV batteries, recyclers use two main methods: pyrometallurgy and hydrometallurgy. In pyrometallurgy, recyclers shred a battery cell and then burn it into a slag, or a charred mass of plastic, metals, and glues. Several methods, including more burning, can be used to extract the metals. In pyrometallurgy, the recycler does not need to know the battery's design to move forward. However, it is a very energy-intensive process.

In contrast, hydrometallurgy dissolves battery materials in acid, which creates a soupy, metal mixture. Hydrometallurgy can extract materials that are difficult to recover through burning, but the process can involve hazardous chemicals. And recovering metals from the soupy mix can be difficult. To make it easier, scientists are testing compounds that could dissolve some battery metals but leave others in solid form, which would make them easier to extract. Both processes, however, produce significant amounts of waste and release greenhouse gases.

Although EVs produce fewer life cycle emissions than gasoline-powered cars, they start their life cycle with a heavier carbon footprint, primarily due to battery production. A 2023 report from Kearney, a global management consulting firm, found that EV supply chain emissions—generated during the vehicle's production and delivery—were 35 to 50 percent higher than those for a comparable internal combustion engine vehicle. "The largest footprint comes from batteries, steel and iron, and aluminum used in vehicles, more specifically the amount and type of energy used in manufacturing,"[34] the study says. As demand for EVs increases, automakers will need to produce and deliver EVs with clean energy to improve overall sustainability.

CHAPTER FOUR

Charging Electric Vehicles

Electric vehicles do not run on gasoline or diesel fuel and do not directly emit greenhouse gases when driven. Yet that does not mean EVs are a completely green transportation solution. A significant source of emissions from EVs comes from the electricity used to power their batteries.

Electric Power and Fossil Fuels

Electricity is an essential source of energy worldwide. Electricity powers homes, businesses, and industry. It also powers EVs. However, generating electricity is a significant source of greenhouse gas emissions in the United States and worldwide. In the United States, the electric power sector includes generating, transmitting, and distributing electricity. In 2021, the US electric power sector generated 25 percent of greenhouse gas emissions, according to a US Environmental Protection Agency report, second only to the transportation sector (28 percent).

Carbon dioxide accounts for the largest percentage of greenhouse gas emissions that result from the production of electric power. This is because most US power plants burn fossil fuels to generate electricity. The type of fossil fuel, such as coal, oil, or natural gas, burned to generate electricity impacts the amount of greenhouse gas emissions released. Coal is a cheap and plentiful energy source, but it is more carbon intensive than oil or natural gas. A carbon-intensive energy source has more carbon than other fossil fuels and produces more carbon dioxide when burned.

Fossil fuels are made from decayed organic materials, which contain carbon-based molecules. For example, coal formed when plants growing in and near swamps died and slowly decomposed underwater. The bacteria and chemicals in the water reacted with the decaying plant matter to form peat. Over time, the peat was buried under layers of sediment, water, and minerals, which added pressure. "When organic matter is buried in sediments, it gets cooked at higher temperatures,"[35] says Shuhei Ono, an MIT professor of geochemistry. The pressure and heat spurred chemical reactions in the peat, which broke down organic molecules and led to a higher concentration of carbon. The peat became coal. Typically, the more pressure and heat added as coal forms, the more carbon it holds.

Burning fossil fuels produces a chemical reaction that releases heat energy. "This is the energy we use for power generation or moving cars, and doing all the things that we do with fossil fuels," explains Gregory Stephanopoulos, an MIT professor of chemical engineering. When fossil fuels burn, oxygen in the air reacts with carbon and hydrogen in the fuel. These reactions form carbon dioxide and water vapor. Because coal has a higher proportion

A Tesla charging station in California. A significant cause of emissions related to EVs comes from the generation of electricity to power their batteries.

of carbon, it releases more carbon molecules and creates more carbon dioxide when burned. In comparison, when oil and natural gas are burned, "mainly the hydrogens . . . will burn and generate energy, not the carbons,"[36] Stephanopoulos says.

Because coal is more carbon intensive than other fossil fuels, it produces more carbon dioxide emissions when burned and is considered a dirty fossil fuel. Although fossil fuels such as oil and natural gas produce fewer emissions than coal, they still produce significant amounts of harmful carbon dioxide. In addition, the burning of natural gas releases methane, a greenhouse gas that warms the atmosphere more than carbon dioxide does.

Therefore, the environmental impact of EVs must account for how the electricity that powers them is produced. Engineer Graham Conway explains that an EV with a small battery pack that can be charged with solar panels is "absolutely without a question going to be cleaner than an internal combustion engine." However, most EVs are charged by charging stations connected to the electrical grid where their owners live. When the grid uses fossil fuels to produce electricity, the climate benefits of EVs drop. "Mainly, it just comes down to how clean the grid is and when people are able to charge,"[37] Conway says.

"Mainly, it just comes down to how clean the grid is and when people are able to charge."[37]

—Graham Conway, principal engineer at Southwest Research Institute

Norway's Clean Charging

Norway, Europe's largest EV market, has demonstrated how the adoption of EVs can be beneficial to people, communities, and the environment. Battery-powered EVs made up 79 percent of Norway's new passenger car registrations in 2022. When PHEVs are included, that number increases to 87 percent of new car registrations. The country plans to end the sale of new internal combustion engine cars by 2025.

The many EVs on Norway's roads are charged with electricity generated almost entirely by renewable energy sources. Norway generates approximately 96 percent of its electricity with hydropower, which is a noncarbon, renewable energy source. Using hydropower to generate electricity often means building dams in rivers and creating artificial lakes, which can impact local ecosystems and surroundings. However, Norway's natural topography with steep valleys and rivers enables hydropower development with minimal impact on the landscape. "Many hydropower plants in Norway are built on existing lakes, so there is not much need to inundate large land areas or displace people,"[38] says Atle Harby, a research scientist who studies hydropower's environmental impact.

Harby sees hydropower as a vital part of a clean electric future. He says,

> As long as we build the power plants in the right place, take the right considerations, and run them properly, hydropower can be our largest and most important source of renewable energy for years to come.
>
> Moreover, reservoir-based hydropower can produce electricity based on demand, as opposed to wind and solar power, which can only produce when the wind blows and the sun shines. Hydropower will therefore be essential to integrating other renewables.[39]

This photo shows a hydroelectric power plant in Norway. The majority of the country's electricity comes from hydropower.

Hydropower

Hydropower is energy created from moving water. It is the largest source of renewable energy worldwide, according to the International Energy Agency. Hydropower generates more electricity than all other renewable energy sources combined. Hydropower solutions can also store thousands of hours of energy in reservoirs. Some hydropower plants can generate energy on demand, complementing intermittent sources like wind or solar power. At night or when there is no strong wind, hydropower can supply the energy needed so there are no gaps in the power grid. Currently, the United States generates about 6 percent of its electricity from hydropower, often from large reservoir-based power plants. About half of total US hydropower generation occurs in Washington, Oregon, and California. Washington's Grand Coulee Dam is the country's largest hydropower facility.

As more EVs have been adopted and powered with clean electricity, greenhouse gas emissions in Oslo, Norway's capital city, dropped by 30 percent between 2009 and 2023. The city is quieter thanks to fewer noisy internal combustion engines. And the air is noticeably cleaner. Nitrogen oxides are a harmful by-product of burning gasoline and diesel fuels and cause smog, asthma, and other harmful health effects. Levels of nitrogen oxides in Oslo's air have dropped sharply as more people have switched to EVs. "We are on the verge of solving the NO_X [nitrogen oxides] problem,"[40] says Tobias Wolf, Oslo's chief engineer for air quality.

Electricity Generation in the United States

When EVs are powered by electricity generated by burning fossil fuels, particularly coal, the environmental benefits are limited. In the United States, fossil fuels are the primary source of generating electricity, producing about 60 percent of electricity in 2022, according to the US Energy Information Administration. Of those fossil fuels, natural gas was the largest source of electricity (40 percent), followed by coal (20 percent) and oil (1 percent). "If we're comparing just coal, oil, and natural gas, the three fossil fuels—natural gas would have the lowest carbon intensity of those three options,"[41] says Jessika Trancik, a professor at MIT's Institute for Data, Systems, and Society. In addition to fossil fuels, the United

Nuclear Power Plants

Nuclear power plants can also produce electricity to power EVs. When a large atom splits into two smaller atoms during nuclear fission, much energy is released as heat. Nuclear power plants use that heat to boil water and produce steam. The steam spins large turbine blades that crank generators and produce electricity. Since 1990, nuclear power plants have generated about 20 percent of US electricity. Unlike fossil fuel power plants, nuclear plants do not emit carbon dioxide or air pollution to generate electricity. However, nuclear power plants have other environmental concerns. Using nuclear energy to generate electricity creates radioactive waste. This waste can remain radioactive, threatening human health for thousands of years.

States produced electricity from nuclear energy (18 percent) and renewable sources (21 percent) in 2022.

Trancik, who has researched climate solutions and greenhouse gas emissions, says that although electricity generated by natural gas is cleaner than electricity from coal, it is still not as climate friendly as electricity produced by solar, wind, or other renewable energy sources. The cleaner the electricity grid, the cleaner EVs can be. "If the grid transitions to a combination of solar energy, wind energy and other low carbon sources, then that's going to make the electric vehicles that much greener than the internal combustion engine vehicles,"[42] Trancik explains.

The Impact on Life Cycle Emissions

A 2022 lifespan study of EV emissions, conducted by researchers at the University of Michigan and sponsored by the Ford Motor Company, shows how important electricity sources are. The study found that EVs, from passenger cars to light trucks, created approximately one-third of the emissions that comparable gasoline-powered vehicles did, from manufacturing to battery disposal.

However, the study also found that electricity generation significantly impacted an EV's lifetime emissions. In the study, seventy-eight out of the three thousand US counties studied experienced greater lifetime emissions from EVs than from gasoline-powered cars. In these counties, electricity was generated by coal. "Coal tends to be the critical factor," says Jeremy Michalek, a professor of engineering at Carnegie Mellon University. "If you've got electric cars in Pittsburgh that are being plugged in at night and leading nearby coal plants to burn more coal to charge them, then the climate benefits won't be as great, and you can even get more air pollution."[43]

However, the study's researchers expect EV emissions to drop as electricity generation becomes more sustainable. "In the future, BEV emissions will decrease due to the retirement of coal plants and the increase in renewable energy sources. Our message is that we need to accelerate the transition to battery electric vehicles,"[44] says the study's lead author, Greg Keoleian, director of the Center for Sustainable Systems at the University of Michigan.

> **"In the future, BEV emissions will decrease due to the retirement of coal plants and the increase in renewable energy sources. Our message is that we need to accelerate the transition to battery electric vehicles."[44]**
>
> **—Greg Keoleian, director of the Center for Sustainable Systems at the University of Michigan**

Cleaning Up the Grid

Many countries, including the United States, have recognized the impact of their electric grids on greenhouse gas emissions. They are actively working to clean up their grids and transition to cleaner sources of electricity. Utility companies across the United States have retired hundreds of coal-fired power plants and replaced them with sources of electricity with lower emissions, including natural gas and nuclear, wind, and solar power. Between 2011 and 2022, the United States cut its use of coal to generate electricity by more than half, according to the Institute for Energy Economics and Financial Analysis (IEEFA). "This milestone is another clear sign of the ongoing and deep restructuring of the US coal industry, as demand for the fuel continues to drop quickly,"[45] says Seth Feaster, an IEEFA energy data analyst. The United States has not built a new coal power plant in over ten years.

Numerous retired coal-fired power plants are being repurposed as renewable energy projects. The transition to renewable sources for electricity generation is easier because the plants are already connected to the country's power grid. Instead of building miles of costly towers and wires to connect power plants to customers, repurposing these plants into renewable energy projects allows them to plug into the existing connections to transmit cleaner electricity. For example, at least nine coal-fired power plants in Illinois will be turned into solar farms and battery storage facilities by 2027. In Massachusetts and New Jersey, two retired coal-fired plants connect offshore wind turbines to local electric grids along the East Coast. Similar projects to repurpose retired coal power plants are in process in several other states, including Nevada, New Mexico, Colorado, and Nebraska. "A silver lining of having had all of these dirty power plants is that now, we have fairly robust transmission lines in those places. That's a huge asset,"[46] says Jack Darin, director of the Illinois chapter of the Sierra Club, an environmental advocacy group. Many of the old coal-fired power plants also have substations that can be used to convert electricity into different voltages that can be used in homes and businesses.

In a number of places around the world, retired coal-fired power plants have been repurposed as renewable energy projects. This photo shows a coal-fired power plant in the United Kingdom that has storage tanks for biofuel, which is burned instead of coal.

Nuclear power operators are also looking to repurpose retired coal power plants. For example, TerraPower, a nuclear power venture, is building an advanced nuclear reactor next to a retiring coal plant in Wyoming. The nuclear reactor will be able to use the coal plant's existing electrical grid connection and its cooling system. "In a way, it'd be a real shame not to make use of those coal plants,"[47] says Chris Levesque, TerraPower's president.

As more electric power is generated by cleaner and renewable energy sources, the cleaner EVs will be over their lifetime. "The reason electric vehicles look like an appealing climate solution is that if we can make our grids zero-carbon, then vehicle emissions drop way, way down. Whereas even the best hybrids that burn gasoline will always have a baseline of emissions they can't go below,"[48] says Trancik.

> "The reason electric vehicles look like an appealing climate solution is that if we can make our grids zero-carbon, then vehicle emissions drop way, way down."[48]
>
> —Jessika Trancik, MIT professor of engineering systems

Charging Stations

Like many electronic devices, EVs and PHEVs connect to a charging station to recharge their batteries. The EV charging station is connected to the electric grid. It delivers electricity to the vehicle, just like any other device plugged into an electrical outlet. For drivers to adopt EVs, charging them must be as easy and convenient as filling up a gas tank at the neighborhood gas station. To achieve this goal, millions of new charging stations will be needed. An analysis by the National Renewable Energy Laboratory estimates that the United States will need an additional 28 million charging stations by 2030 to support an estimated 33 million EVs driving on the road.

An increase of this magnitude in charging stations can impact local communities and environments. Sometimes, building new stations can disrupt natural wildlife habitats and ecosystems, especially if they are built in areas with sensitive ecosystems. As the number of EVs plugging into the electrical grid increases, there is a risk of the grid becoming overloaded, particularly during peak charging times. To reduce this risk, charging infrastructure may need to be designed and upgraded to support the increased electricity demand.

Improving the efficiency of EV charging stations will also improve sustainability. More efficient charging stations use less electricity to charge EVs, which reduces their overall carbon footprint. More efficient charging also reduces charging time, making EVs more appealing to drivers.

Overall, EVs produce significantly less harmful emissions than gasoline-powered cars do. Yet EV benefits depend greatly on how much coal and other fossil fuels are burned to charge them. Until the electric grids that power EVs get significantly cleaner, EVs will not be emissions-free.

CHAPTER FIVE

Improving Electric Vehicle Sustainability

Experts generally agree that EVs are a greener option than traditional gasoline-powered vehicles. However, EVs are not without drawbacks and—depending on the materials used, how they are manufactured, and how they are charged—have an environmental impact. Recognizing that EVs can be better for the environment, several initiatives and research projects are under way worldwide to make EVs more sustainable and environmentally friendly.

Cobalt-Free Batteries

The use of cobalt in EV lithium-ion batteries is problematic in several ways. Much of the world's cobalt is mined in areas with few environmental regulations. As a result, cobalt mining has caused increased pollution, soil and water contamination, and habitat destruction. Also, cobalt mining has been linked to unsafe working conditions, human rights abuses, and harm to human health. Beyond these environmental and ethical problems, cobalt is also expensive and vulnerable to disruptions in the supply chain. "Cobalt batteries can store a lot of energy, and they have all of [the] features that people care about in terms of performance, but they have the issue of not being widely available, and the cost fluctuates broadly with commodity prices. And, as you transition to a much higher proportion of electrified vehicles in the consumer market, it's certainly going to get more expensive,"[49] says Mircea Dincă, a professor at MIT.

In response, scientists and the EV industry are developing alternative battery designs to reduce and eliminate reliance on cobalt. For example, some automakers have started using lithium iron phosphate (LFP) batteries in EVs. LFP batteries are very stable, have a long lifespan, and are generally more available and cheaper to produce. However, the drawback of LFP batteries is that they store about 30 percent less energy than cobalt batteries of the same size.

Researchers at the University of Tokyo have built a cobalt-free lithium-ion battery prototype. The researchers used lithium, nickel, manganese, silicon, and oxygen to create the battery's electrodes. This combination of elements allows the battery to withstand higher voltages. Higher voltages push more electricity to an electronic device. The researchers also developed a new electrolyte, which they hope will help prevent the battery's components from breaking down early. The cobalt-free battery prototype can store about 60 percent more energy than similar-sized alternatives. It also retains 80 percent of its storage capacity after one thousand charge and discharge cycles. The researchers plan to test and monitor how the cobalt-free battery performs over several years. "We will consider ways to collaborate with companies interested in commercializing the technology, including through licensing,"[50] says University of Tokyo professor Atsuo Yamada.

At MIT, researchers are developing a cobalt-free lithium-ion battery using organic materials. While ecologically appealing, scientists have struggled in previous efforts to develop a successful battery out of organic materials. However, the MIT project seems to yield a multilayered, fully organic material that is conductive and highly stable. The researchers replaced the cobalt in a battery cathode—the negative terminal of an EV lithium-ion battery—with layers of organic molecules composed of carbon, hydrogen, oxygen, and nitrogen. In a 2024 study, MIT researchers showed that the organic material could conduct electricity at a similar rate as cobalt lithium-ion batteries and could be produced at a much lower cost. The cobalt-free battery also had comparable energy storage capacity and could be charged faster than the cobalt batteries. "I think this material could have a big impact because it works really well. It is already competitive with incumbent technologies. And it can save a lot of the cost and pain and environmental issues related to mining the metals that currently go into batteries,"[51] says Dincă.

Cleaner Lithium Production

Lithium-ion batteries power today's EVs because they can store a large amount of electrical energy in a smaller, lighter package compared to other types of batteries. Also, lithium-ion batteries perform well at high temperatures and can handle low temperatures without damage. However, mining lithium has environmental costs. Mining operations disturb landscapes and habitats and use valuable water resources, and waste from mining operations can contaminate water supplies in nearby communities.

The EV industry is trying to develop new battery designs that reduce reliance on cobalt. This 2023 photo shows Chinese battery manufacturer Contemporary Amperex Technology Co., Ltd., demonstrating a new battery design.

Developing cleaner methods of producing lithium will improve EV sustainability, especially as more EVs hit the road in the coming years. In 2021 British Lithium (a producer of lithium carbonate) announced that it had developed a low-energy, chemical-free process to physically separate mica, a mineral that contains lithium, from granite bedrock. Granite is one of the most common rocks on Earth's surface, and the new process would reduce environmental harm caused by lithium production.

> "At the moment, we will be the only lithium producer in the world to be quarrying and refining on one site, which adds to the sustainability of the project."[52]
>
> —Roderick Smith, British Lithium's director

In 2022, British Lithium announced that it had successfully piloted its new lithium development process at a test plant in the United Kingdom. Using patented technology, plant workers performed each step in the production process, from quarrying the granite to purifying the lithium. Once the process is refined, British Lithium plans to build a full-scale plant. "Our goal is to produce 21,000 tonnes [23,149 tons] of battery-grade lithium carbonate each year. At the moment, we will be the only lithium producer in the world to be quarrying and refining on one site, which adds to the sustainability of the project,"[52] says Roderick Smith, British Lithium's director.

Reuse: A Second Life

Other efforts to improve EV sustainability focus on new ways to reuse EV batteries. A battery enters its second life after it is no longer suitable for its original purpose but can still be used in some new way. EV batteries that are no longer useful for cars and trucks can be reused in other vehicles that do not travel long distances, such as golf carts. Another idea is to repurpose them for other energy storage needs, such as storing energy for rooftop solar grids or other backup storage needs. "There's definitely some potential in the utility sector, especially in terms of grid backup storage . . . even though [old EV batteries] have lost, say, 20% of their original capacity . . . when you're talking about grid storage that can still be a perfectly usable battery for several more years,"[53] says the NRDC's Jordan Brinn.

However, repurposing EV batteries for storage on the electric grid is still a new practice, and some challenges will need to be addressed before it becomes commonplace. For example, an EV battery cannot simply be removed from a vehicle and immediately connected to the electric grid or other new use. The battery must be evaluated, tested, and updated before reusing. Additionally, many manufacturers design their own EV batteries, which could make it complicated to gain access to those proprietary designs when determining how the batteries work and how best to use them in an electric grid.

New Recycling Efforts

Few lithium-ion batteries are recycled, with some estimates at less than 5 percent. In comparison, nearly all lead-acid batteries (99 percent) are recycled. As more EVs hit the road, programs to reuse and recycle lithium-ion batteries will reduce the potential environmental harm of producing and disposing of batteries.

A Circular Economy

Several EV manufacturers are embracing circular economy practices to improve sustainability. For EVs, a circular economy involves designing vehicles and batteries so they can be quickly and efficiently taken apart and recycled. Then, the recycled materials are used in new vehicles as much as possible.

EV automaker Tesla is committed to circular economy practices. Tesla uses recycled materials in its vehicles, including aluminum, copper, plastic, and steel. To recycle its batteries, the company works with third-party recyclers and is also developing in-house battery recycling technology. "Tesla has an established internal ecosystem to remanufacture batteries coming from the field to our service centers. We actively implement circular economy principles," the company states in its 2020 Impact Report. Tesla plans to recover and reuse up to 92 percent of raw metals in new batteries. It is also exploring ways to reuse its batteries for backup storage applications.

Quoted in Deanne Toto, "Tesla Prioritizes Raw Material Reuse," Recycling Today, August 11, 2021. www.recyclingtoday.com.

Some companies are developing ways to recycle EV batteries sustainably. According to Brinn, when an EV battery is recycled, 95 percent of its minerals can be reused in new batteries. Nevada-based Redwood Materials takes end-of-life EV batteries and scrap materials from automobile factories and turns them into raw materials and components for new EV batteries. Redwood uses processes such as pyrometallurgy and hydrometallurgy. They recapture cobalt, copper, nickel, and other raw materials from the used batteries and recycle them for use in new batteries.

Redwood has partnered with automakers such as Toyota to provide a domestic source of battery raw materials. "Working with Redwood Materials, we are creating a circular supply chain to optimize logistics, expand refining, and ensure that the valuable metals recovered can be reintroduced into our future vehicles," says Christopher Yang, vice president of Toyota Motor North America. "Accelerating our recycling efforts and domestic component procurement gets us closer to our ultimate goal of creating a closed-loop battery ecosystem that will become increasingly important as we add more vehicles with batteries to roads across North America."[54]

States Ban Gasoline Cars

To speed the transition to EVs, several US states have banned the sales of new gasoline-powered cars after 2035, or they plan to do so. In these states, new car sales must be zero-emission vehicles, such as EVs or some PHEVs. Drivers could continue to own and operate traditional gasoline cars and buy used gasoline cars, but automakers and car dealerships would be prohibited from selling new ones. In 2022, California was the first state to adopt the rule to require all new car sales be zero-emission vehicles by 2035. As of March 2024, other states that have adopted or plan to adopt this ban included Maryland, Rhode Island, Massachusetts, New Jersey, New York, Oregon, and Washington, as well as the District of Columbia. In March 2023, Maryland's governor, Wes Moore, announced his state's plan to eliminate sales of new gasoline-powered cars. "It's a major step in the state's acceleration to improve air quality and combat the effects of climate change," he said.

Quoted in Pete Grieve, "8 States Now Plan to Ban Gas-Powered Car Sales," *Money*, March 21, 2024. https://money.com.

In Sweden, researchers have developed a more efficient way of recycling old EV batteries, allowing greater recovery of valuable metals, including 100 percent of the aluminum and 98 percent of the lithium. The recycling process does not use expensive or harmful chemicals. Instead, researchers dissolve the EV battery's metals in an organic liquid called oxalic acid, which is found in plants such as spinach and rhubarb. "Our method is a promising new route for battery recycling—a route that definitely warrants further exploration,"[55] says Léa Rouquette, a doctoral student at Sweden's Chalmers University of Technology. "As the method can be scaled up, we hope it can be used in industry in future years,"[56] says research leader Martina Petranikova.

Improving EV Charging

Researchers are also developing technologies to improve EV charging and make it more sustainable. At the 2023 North American International Auto Show in Detroit, engineer Jim Bardia unveiled a scale model of his patented Wind & Solar Tower EV charging station, which can provide fast EV charging without being connected to the grid. "The U.S. electric grid needs strengthening because it is being asked to deliver far more energy than ever before. But we can't be spending billions of dollars to build additional power plants that will increase pollution by burning more fossil fuels,"[57] says Bardia.

> **"Only renewable energy can provide EV charges without stressing the grid and dirtying the air."[58]**
>
> —Jim Bardia, engineer and inventor

The tower combines a vertical wind turbine that can catch wind from any direction with solar panels on top of the turbine tower. The self-powered tower generates electricity from the wind and sun. The tower can charge six EVs simultaneously and generates enough electricity to power more than ninety-four hundred EVs annually. Because the tower does not need to be connected to the grid, it can be installed anywhere there is enough space, even in remote locations. "Only renewable energy can provide EV charges without stressing the grid and dirtying the air," Bardia says. "Fortunately, 'clean' charging is a choice. Sooner or later, emission-free charging will become standard—and the sooner that happens, the better for our grid and our health."[58]

Vehicle to Grid

As the demand for EVs and electric charging increases, the load on power grids is projected to increase by as much as 38 percent by 2050, according to a US Department of Energy study. With vehicle-to-grid (V2G) technology, EVs and their charging stations can be part of the solution to meet the country's electricity needs. Using bidirectional charging stations, EVs charge during times of low electricity demand. Then, during peak electricity demand hours, EVs send energy stored in the car batteries back to the grid to help meet demand. V2G technology could also provide backup power for EV owners when other sources are unavailable. For example, a home with solar power could use stored energy from an EV to provide electricity at night as needed.

The Nissan Leaf is one of the first EV models to use V2G technology. Joseph Evans, the owner of a vineyard in Australia's Barossa Valley, drives his Leaf to make wine deliveries to local restaurants. He recharges the EV through solar panels at his home. Then Evans plugs his Leaf into a V2G charger and uses the energy stored in the EV battery to power his home overnight. In the morning, he recharges the car with solar power. With its V2G technology, the Leaf provides enough energy for Evans's living, heating, and cooling energy needs. He also returns any excess energy to the grid, earning a little money. Evans uses a simple app on his phone to charge or discharge power from his car, providing power for his home and helping Australia's power grid. "This is a game-changer, and I wanted to be right at the front of the queue to have V2G installed. It makes me entirely self-sufficient with my power needs, makes my home and business more sustainable, and it's so easy to use,"[59] says Evans.

Dynamic Charging

Dynamic charging technology is another emerging technology that can make EVs more sustainable. With dynamic charging, EVs charge in motion using overhead power lines or electrified roads. Dynamic charging would make long-distance EV travel more practical and eliminate the need to stop periodically to charge the vehicle's battery.

In a wireless electric charging road in Detroit, Michigan, cars are charged by copper coils in the roadway. The location of the coils is marked with white dots.

In 2023 the first US wireless electric charging road was tested in Detroit, Michigan. The pilot project uses wireless charging technology built by Electreon, an Israel-based EV wireless charging solutions developer, to charge EVs as they drive about a quarter mile near the city's landmark Michigan Central Station. The EVs have a receiver installed underneath, enabling them to wirelessly charge from copper coils inserted into the roadway. The wireless charging system is activated when a vehicle with a receiver drives over the copper coils. Receivers can be installed under any EV, including cars, vans, trucks, and buses. "We'll demonstrate how wireless charging unlocks widespread EV adoption, addressing limited range, grid limitations, and battery size and costs. This project paves the way for a zero-emission mobility future, where EVs are the norm, not the exception,"[60] says Stefan Tongur, Electreon's vice president of business development.

"Contrary to some claims, electric car adoption is not a fool's errand; it will slash emissions in the long run and accelerate the energy transition."[61]

—Abhishek Murali, Rystad Energy analyst

The sustainability of EVs depends heavily on how they are manufactured and charged. In particular, the production of EV batteries can cause environmental and human rights challenges. However, most experts agree that despite these challenges, EVs will have a positive environmental impact over their lifetime. According to analyst Abhishek Murali of Rystad Energy, a business research company,

> Overall, battery electric vehicles are clearly the right technology to reduce emissions in the transportation sector. Switching to a BEV will reduce long-term emissions despite a larger environmental impact at the beginning of the vehicle's life. Contrary to some claims, electric car adoption is not a fool's errand; it will slash emissions in the long run and accelerate the energy transition.[61]

SOURCE NOTES

Introduction: Paving the Way for Electric Vehicles

1. Dara Khosrowshahi, "Driving a Green Recovery," Uber Newsroom, September 8, 2020. www.uber.com.
2. Quoted in Tiah Shepherd, "Uber Is Working to Have Zero-Emissions by 2030 and These Drivers Want to Tell You About It," MassLive, May 24, 2023. www.masslive.com.
3. Akiko Hara, "I Love My Electric Car but I Didn't Realize My Life Would Revolve Around Charging It," CBC, May 31, 2023. www.cbc.ca.
4. Quoted in Volvo, "Volvo Cars to Be Fully Electric by 2030," Press Release, March 2, 2021. www.media.volvocars.com.
5. Quoted in Yvonne Bertucci zum Tobel, "How Green Are Electric Vehicles? Well, That Depends," WUSF, September 25, 2022. www.wusf.org.

Chapter One: What Are Electric Vehicles?

6. Quoted in Kelley Blue Book, "Americans Buy Nearly 1.2 Million Electric Vehicles to Hit Record in 2023, According to Latest Kelley Blue Book Data," January 16, 2024. https://mediaroom.kbb.
7. Quoted in Jillian Mackenzie and Jeff Turrentine, "Air Pollution: Everything You Need to Know," Natural Resources Defense Council, October 31, 2023. www.nrdc.org.
8. Quoted in Mackenzie and Turrentine, "Air Pollution."
9. Quoted in Andrew Gregory, "Air Pollution from Fossil Fuels 'Kills 5 Million People a Year,'" *The Guardian,* November 29, 2023. www.theguardian.com.
10. Quoted in Iris Crawford, "How Much CO_2 Is Emitted by Manufacturing Batteries?," MIT Climate Portal, July 15, 2022. https://climate.mit.edu.
11. Quoted in Crawford, "How Much CO_2 Is Emitted by Manufacturing Batteries?"
12. Quoted in Andrew Moseman, "Are Electric Vehicles Definitely Better for the Climate than Gas-Powered Cars?," MIT Climate Portal, October 13, 2022. https://climate.mit.edu.

Chapter Two: Mining for Raw Materials

13. Quoted in Aaron Steckelberg et al., "The Underbelly of Electric Vehicles," *Washington Post,* April 27, 2023. www.washingtonpost.com.

14. Quoted in Leah Burrows, "Battery Breakthrough for Electric Cars," *Harvard Gazette,* May 12, 2021. https://news.harvard.edu.
15. Quoted in United Nations Environment Programme, "Critical Ecosystems: Congo Basin Peatlands," February 27, 2023. www.unep.org.
16. Quoted in United Nations Environment Programme, "Critical Ecosystems."
17. Quoted in Kara Norton, "Cobalt Powers Our Lives. What Is It—and Why Is It So Controversial?," *National Geographic,* December 21, 2023. www.nationalgeographic.com.
18. Quoted in Terry Gross, "How 'Modern-Day Slavery' in the Congo Powers the Rechargeable Battery Economy," *Fresh Air*, NPR, February 1, 2023. www.npr.org.
19. Quoted in Gross, "How 'Modern-Day Slavery' in the Congo Powers the Rechargeable Battery Economy."
20. Quoted in Gross, "How 'Modern-Day Slavery' in the Congo Powers the Rechargeable Battery Economy."
21. Quoted in Osama Alshantti, "Cobalt Mining in the Democratic Republic of the Congo: The Human and Environmental Costs of the Transition to Green Technology," *Spheres of Influence,* July 22, 2022. https://spheresofinfluence.ca.
22. Quoted in Nicole Greenfield, "Lithium Mining Is Leaving Chile's Indigenous Communities High and Dry (Literally)," Natural Resources Defense Council, April 26, 2022. www.nrdc.org.
23. Quoted in Hiroko Tabuchi and Brad Plumer, "How Green Are Electric Vehicles?," *New York Times,* March 2, 2021. www.nytimes.com.

Chapter Three: The Electric Vehicle Production Process

24. Quoted in Chris Clonts, "Decarbonizing the EV Battery Supply Chain," *Tech Briefs,* June 1, 2023. www.techbriefs.com.
25. Quoted in Jasper Jolly, "Do Electric Cars Really Produce Fewer Carbon Emissions than Petrol or Diesel Vehicles?," *The Guardian,* December 23, 2023. www.theguardian.com.
26. Quoted in Crawford, "How Much CO_2 Is Emitted by Manufacturing Batteries?"
27. Quoted in Joni Auden Land, "Exploding Lithium Batteries Are Causing Fires in Oregon's Landfills," Oregon Public Broadcasting, October 21, 2023. www.opb.org.
28. Quoted in Land, "Exploding Lithium Batteries Are Causing Fires in Oregon's Landfills."
29. Jordan Brinn, *Building Batteries Better: Doing the Best with Less.* New York: Natural Resources Defense Council, 2023. www.nrdc.org.

30. Quoted in Andrew Moseman, "How Well Can Electric Vehicle Batteries Be Recycled?," MIT Climate Portal, September 5, 2023. https://climate.mit.edu.
31. Quoted in Ian Morse, "A Dead Battery Dilemma," *Science,* May 20, 2021. www.science.org.
32. Hydrovolt, "Hydrovolt and Fortum Battery Recycling Join Forces to Drive the Nordic Battery Industry Forward," February 29, 2024. www.hydrovolt.com.
33. Quoted in Moseman, "How Well Can Electric Vehicle Batteries Be Recycled?"
34. Quoted in Patrick George, "EVs 'Are Not Enough': Polestar and Rivian Urge More Drastic Climate Action," The Verge, February 9, 2023. www.theverge.com.

Chapter Four: Charging EVs

35. Quoted in MIT Climate Portal, "Why Does Burning Coal Generate More CO_2 than Oil or Gas?," December 16, 2022. https://climate.mit.edu.
36. Quoted in MIT Climate Portal, "Why Does Burning Coal Generate More CO_2 than Oil or Gas?"
37. Quoted in Bertucci zum Tobel, "How Green Are Electric Vehicles?"
38. Quoted in Business Norway, "How Norway Produces Hydropower with a Minimal Carbon Footprint," March 15, 2023. https://businessnorway.com.
39. Quoted in Business Norway, "How Norway Produces Hydropower with a Minimal Carbon Footprint."
40. Quoted in Jack Ewing, "In Norway, the Electric Vehicle Future Has Already Arrived," *New York Times,* May 8, 2023. www.nytimes.com.
41. Quoted in Bertucci zum Tobel, "How Green Are Electric Vehicles?"
42. Quoted in Bertucci zum Tobel, "How Green Are Electric Vehicles?"
43. Quoted in Tabuchi and Plumer, "How Green Are Electric Vehicles?"
44. Quoted in Eric A. Taub, "E.V.s Start with a Bigger Carbon Footprint. But That Doesn't Last," *New York Times,* October 19, 2022. www.nytimes.com.
45. Quoted in Institute for Energy Economics and Financial Analysis, "The U.S. Is on Track to Close Half of Its Coal-Fired Generation Capacity by 2026," April 3, 2023. https://ieefa.org.
46. Quoted in Elena Shao, "In a Twist, Old Coal Plants Help Deliver Renewable Power. Here's How," *New York Times,* July 15, 2022. www.nytimes.com.
47. Quoted in Shao, "In a Twist, Old Coal Plants Help Deliver Renewable Power."
48. Quoted in Bertucci zum Tobel, "How Green Are Electric Vehicles?"

Chapter Five: Improving EV Sustainability

49. Quoted in Anne Trafton, "Cobalt-Free Batteries Could Power Cars of the Future," MIT News, January 18, 2024. https://news.mit.edu.
50. Quoted in Jota Tsuchiya, "Japanese Scientists Make Better Lithium-Ion Battery Without Cobalt," Nikkei Asia, October 29, 2023. https://asia.nikkei.com.
51. Quoted in Trafton, "Cobalt-Free Batteries Could Power Cars of the Future."
52. Quoted in Lisa Letcher, "Big World Mining First for Cornwall as Electric Car Battery Ingredient Lithium Is Extracted near Roche," Cornwall Live, January 6, 2022. www.cornwalllive.com.
53. Quoted in Kavya Balaraman, "EV Batteries Can Be Repurposed as Grid Storage to Reduce Battery Supply Chain Impacts: Report," Utility Dive, July 11, 2023. www.utilitydive.com.
54. Toyota Motor North America, "Toyota and Redwood Materials Agree to Battery Recycling, Materials Procurement," PR Newswire, November 16, 2023. www.prnewswire.com.
55. Quoted in Rebecca Ann Hughes, "'Promising' New Breakthrough for Recycling EV Batteries Discovered by Swedish Scientists," Euronews, October 17, 2023. www.euronews.com.
56. Quoted in Hughes, "'Promising' New Breakthrough for Recycling EV Batteries Discovered by Swedish Scientists."
57. Quoted in Wind & Solar Tower, "Off-the-Grid, Solar and Wind EV Charger to Make Debut at Detroit Auto Show," September 15, 2023. https://windandsolartower.com.
58. Quoted in Wind & Solar Tower, "Off-the-Grid, Solar and Wind EV Charger to Make Debut at Detroit Auto Show."
59. Quoted in Nissan Australia, "The Vehicle-to-Grid Revolution Has Arrived in Australia," December 22, 2022. www.nissan.com.au.
60. Quoted in Corey Williams, "New Technology Installed beneath Detroit Street Can Charge Electric Vehicles as They Drive," Associated Press, November 29, 2023. https://apnews.com.
61. Quoted in Rystad Energy, "Driving the Energy Transition, EVs Are Simply Better for the Environment," October 2, 2023. www.rystadenergy.com.

ORGANIZATIONS AND WEBSITES

Intergovernmental Panel on Climate Change (IPCC)
www.ipcc.ch
The IPCC is the United Nations body for assessing the science related to climate change. It provides information about many issues related to climate change. Its website provides links to the group's research reports, data, news, and other climate activities.

The International Council on Clean Transportation (ICCT)
www.theicct.org
The ICCT is a nonprofit organization that provides research and technical analysis to environmental regulators. Its website has articles, videos, reports, and more information about electric vehicles.

International Energy Association (IEA)
www.iea.org
The IEA works with countries around the world to shape energy policies for a secure and sustainable future. It provides energy data and analysis to users worldwide. Its website has energy profiles by country, information about fuels and technologies, research reports and analysis, and other energy-related data.

Natural Resources Defense Council (NRDC)
www.nrdc.org
The NRDC is a nonprofit international environmental advocacy group that works to defend the rights to clean air, water, and healthy communities. It provides information about several environmental issues, including climate change and greenhouse gas emissions. The NRDC website provides information about the group's work in various climate change initiatives.

Pew Research Center
www.pewresearch.org
Pew Research Center is a nonpartisan American think tank that provides information on social issues, public opinion, and demographic trends shaping the United States and the world, including climate change. Under research topics, Pew's website offers information, reports, and data about climate, energy, electric vehicles, and the environment.

Plug In America
www.pluginamerica.org
Plug In America is a nonprofit organization that aims to accelerate the transition to plug-in vehicles through education, research, and advocacy. Its website has articles, press releases, and more information about electric vehicles.

United Nations Environment Programme (UNEP)
www.unep.org
UNEP is the arm of the United Nations responsible for coordinating its responses to environmental issues, including climate change. Its website has a section on the group's climate action and the latest climate reports, publications, fact sheets, interactives, and more.

FOR FURTHER RESEARCH

Books

Matt Chandler, *The Tech Behind Electric Cars*. North Mankato, MN: Capstone, 2020.

Robyn Hardyman, *Innovators Improving Transportation*. New York: Lucent, 2020.

Kristina Lyn Heitkamp, *Electric Vehicles*. Lake Elmo, MN: Focus Readers, 2020.

James Taylor, *Electric Cars*. London: Bloomsbury, 2022.

Kevin Wilson, *The Electric Vehicle Revolution: The Past, Present, and Future of EVs*. Beverly, MA: Motorbooks, 2023.

Internet Sources

Jordan Brinn, *Building Batteries Better: Doing the Best with Less*. New York: NRDC, 2023. www.nrdc.org.

Brian Kennedy, Cary Funk, and Alec Tyson, *Majorities of Americans Prioritize Renewable Energy, Back Steps to Address Climate Change*. Washington, DC: Pew Research Center, 2023. www.pewresearch.org.

Ian Morse, "A Dead Battery Dilemma," *Science*, May 20, 2021. www.science.org.

David Reichmuth, Jessica Dunn, and Don Anair, *Driving Cleaner: How Electric Cars and Pickups Beat Gasoline on Lifetime Global Warming Emissions*. Cambridge, MA: Union of Concerned Scientists, 2022. www.ucsusa.org.

Alison Spencer, Stephanie Ross, and Alec Tyson, "How Americans View Electric Vehicles," Pew Research Center, July 13, 2023. www.pewresearch.org.

INDEX